NATURAL WONDERS

Angel Falls

The Highest Waterfall in the World

Galadriel Watson

WEIGL PUBLISHERS INC.

Published by Weigl Publishers Inc.
350 5th Avenue, Suite 3304, PMB 6G
New York, NY 10118-0069
USA

Web site: www.weigl.com

Library of Congress Cataloging-in-Publication Data

Watson, Galadriel Findlay.
  Angel falls : the tallest waterfall in the world / by Galadriel Watson.
    p. cm. — (Natural wonders)
  Includes index.
  ISBN 1-59036-267-5 (lib. bdg. : alk. paper) 1-59036-273-X (pbk.)
  1. Angel Falls (Venezuela)—Juvenile literature. I. Title. II. Natural wonders (Weigl Publishers)
  GB1480.A54W37 2004
  918.7'63—dc22
                    2004013605

Printed in the United States of America
1 2 3 4 5 6 7 8 9 0 08 07 06 05 04

Editorial Services
BookMark Publishing, Inc.

Editor
Heather C. Hudak

Design
Terry Paulhus

Layout
Biner Design

Photo Researcher
Dawn Friedman,
BookMark Publishing, Inc.

Photo Description
Cover: Thousands of years of flowing water has carved Devil's Canyon into Auyán Tepuy.
Title page: The Auyán Tepuy and about forty other tepuys in the Gran Sabana have a reddish sandstone rock.

Photograph Credits

Cover: Angel Falls (James Marshall/CORBIS/MAGMA); **Adrian Warren, Lastrefuge.co.uk:** pages 1, 7, 8, 19, 20, 21, 22, 24; **AP/Wide World Photos:** page 26B (Andres Mata Foundation); **Cortez C. Austin, Jr.:** page 13; **CORBIS/MAGMA:** pages 15 (Underwood & Underwood), 18 (Chris Rainier), 25L (Sally A. Morgan, Ecoscene), 25R (Pablo Corral V); **Wolfgang Kaehler 2004, www.wkaehlerphoto.com:** page 27T; **Photo Researchers, Inc.:** pages 4 (Jacques Jangoux), 6 (Francois Gohier), 10 (Francois Gohier), 11 (Jacques Jangoux), 12 (Jany Sauvanet); **Photos.com:** pages 23L, 23R, 27B, 28; **Photography Collection, Harry Ransom Humanities Research Center, the University of Texas at Austin:** page 14; **Tom Stack & Associates:** page 26T (Joe McDonald).

Contents

A Tumble of Water

Perhaps you have visited Niagara Falls, one of North America's largest waterfalls. Now picture Niagara eighteen times higher. You can begin to imagine the breathtaking sight of the highest waterfall in the world, Venezuela's Angel Falls.

Called *Salto Ángel* in Spanish, Angel Falls sends water tumbling more than 3,212 feet (979 meters) off a mountain cliff. The water falls so far that it makes a deafening roar as it hits the rocks and water below. As people approach Angel Falls from a distance, they say they hear its constant "whoosh" from as far as 3 miles (4.8 kilometers) away.

■ **Angel Falls pours off the edge of a mountain called Auyán Tepuy. The falls are fed by the Churún River.**

Angel Falls Facts:

- Angel Falls stands 3,212 feet (979 m) high, the highest waterfall in the world. It is almost twice as high as the world's tallest building.

- Its longest uninterrupted drop is 2,648 feet (807 m)—also the highest in the world.

- Auyán Tepuy stands 8,400 feet (2,560 m) above sea level.

- Angel Falls is part of Venezuela's Canaima National Park. The park features many other mountains and waterfalls.

Angel Falls Locator

Where in the World?

Angel Falls is located in Venezuela, one of the most northern countries in South America. The waterfall and its mountain are part of the Gran Sabana, where rolling **savannah** grasslands are interrupted by huge *tepuys* (flat-topped mountains). The Gran Sabana is part of the larger Guayana Highlands region. The highlands stretch from Venezuela to the southeast and cross several countries' borders.

The rainy season in the Gran Sabana lasts from May to November. Clouds blow in from the Atlantic Ocean, causing huge amounts of rain to fall on the region. These sudden downpours help to feed the many rivers that crisscross the land. Some of the rivers eventually empty at waterfalls. There are hundreds of waterfalls in the region, but none is as amazing as Angel Falls.

Some 965,000 square miles (2.5 million sq km) of savannah cover Venezuela and other South American countries.

The Lost World

Angel Falls may be the highest waterfall, but nearby Roraima Tepuy is the highest mountain in the Guayana Highlands. The stunning mountain is surrounded by jungles containing strange and rare wildlife. Many plants that grow here are found no place else on Earth.

Some people exploring Roraima feel as if they have stepped into a prehistoric age. That very idea inspired British author Sir Arthur Conan Doyle to write his 1912 novel *The Lost World*. In the book, a group of explorers discover a land of dinosaurs and ape-men on the mountain. Today, people often refer to the entire Gran Sabana as the "lost world."

Roraima Tepuy's immense flat top ranges for 26 square miles (67 sq km).

A Trip Back in Time

Just how did these amazing mountains take their shape? About 1.8 billion years ago, South America was part of a much larger continent that sat where Africa is today. Then, about 180 million years ago, Earth's **tectonic plates** made a huge shift. The large continent split into smaller pieces. One of those pieces traveled to the west and became South America.

About 3 to 4 million years ago, the moving continent caused violent shifting below ground. In some spots, the earth pushed upward, forcing large pieces of rock to the surface. This is how the tepuys we see today were originally formed. In the time that has passed, wind and water have **eroded** the land further. Erosion has carved amazing, interesting shapes into the rocky surfaces.

■ Water from Angel Falls erodes the rocky side and base of Auyán Tepuy.

Puzzler

South America was once part of a "supercontinent," which **geologists** call Gondwana, or Gondwanaland. Over time, South America separated from Gondwana, becoming its own continent. When Gondwana separated, five continents formed.

Q Which continents formed when Gondwana separated?

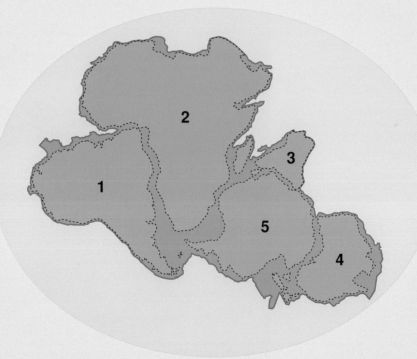

 1. South America 2. Africa 3. India 4. Australia 5. Antarctica

A Challenge to Plant Life

Plants can have a difficult time growing in some areas of the Gran Sabana. Much of the soil is poor quality because the nearby rocks provide few **minerals**. The soil is also quite old and is often harmed by the climate. Another challenge to plant life is that people frequently burn trees and plants.

There are, however, areas of the Gran Sabana where rich soil allows vibrant plant life to grow. Near rivers and streams, tropical forests host an incredible array of plants. Giant palms reach the sky, and water hyacinths float on the rivers. Fruits, such as wild pineapples, are found here. Plants, such as sundew, sun pitcher, and bladderwort, are **carnivorous**. They survive by eating insects.

■ **The poor soil of the savannah cannot support much plant life other than certain types of grasses.**

Outstanding Orchids

Every **species** of orchid features a spectacularly colored and shaped flower. Orchid-lovers around the world take pains to grow these flowers. In most natural environments, orchids are difficult to grow.

The Gran Sabana, however, is a paradise of orchids. Here, orchids grow by the thousands. As expected, they flourish in the humid jungle areas near rivers and waterfalls. Surprisingly, orchids also thrive in rocky areas. Orchid fans travel to the Gran Sabana just to look at these brilliant flowers.

The epidendrum is one of 500 to 700 orchid species that grow in the Gran Sabana.

Wonderful Wildlife

In the forest areas near Angel Falls, visitors see and hear a fascinating community of animals. Bird calls fill the air throughout the forests. From toucans to eagles, there are more than three times as many bird species as mammal species in the Gran Sabana.

Along with the birds, many other animals, such as jaguars, jaguarundies, and monkeys, live in the forest. The three-toed sloth is one of the most interesting tree-dwelling creatures of the Gran Sabana. These mammals sleep quite a bit, sometimes 18 hours a day. Some sloths live in the same tree for their entire lives.

Many animals in the region can be dangerous, so visitors must be alert. Caimans, cousins of the alligator, slither through river waters. Razor-toothed piranhas also swim about, hunting for prey. Ants may be tiny, but they are strong in number. They band together and attack any person or animal that touches the tree that hosts their nest.

The three-toed sloth's claws are large and round enough to hook around tree limbs. They can hang from trees for hours.

The Biggest of the Big

Some very large animals make their homes in the Gran Sabana.

- King vultures have wingspans of more than 6 feet (1.8 m).
- Giant anteaters consume more than 30,000 ants every day.
- Anacondas are one of the largest snakes in the world.
- Giant otters can grow to 6 feet (1.8 m) long.

The largest rodent in the world, the capybara, lives in the Gran Sabana.

Measuring the Falls

Who was the first person to measure Angel Falls and declare it the highest waterfall in the world? In 1949, an American journalist named Ruth Robertson accomplished this feat.

Four previous **expeditions** had failed to reach the falls. By canoe and on foot, Robertson's team carried cameras, electric generators, radios, and other heavy equipment to the base of the falls. Other than **indigenous** peoples who lived there, Robertson and her crew were the first humans to see the waterfall from the jungle below. She wrote a detailed journal, made maps of the area, and snapped hundreds of photographs. From her pictures and maps, she was able to determine the true height of the falls. Her story was published in *National Geographic* magazine. Robertson's photos were the first glimpse of Angel Falls for many people around the world.

■ **Ruth Robertson and her 1949 expedition team pose proudly with Angel Falls in the background.**

Biography

Jimmie Angel (1899–1956)

Jimmie Angel's goal was gold, but instead he stumbled upon the world's highest waterfall. Born in Missouri, Jimmie believed Auyán Tepuy was the home of a lost river of gold. While searching the area by plane in 1933, he first saw the falls. Jimmie did not land the plane, but he did tell his friends about the amazing waterfall he spotted. A few years later, one of his friends said the waterfall should be named Angel Falls, after Jimmie.

Jimmie Angel returned to the Auyán Tepuy in 1937, intending to land on top of Auyán Tepuy and again search for gold. With his wife and several companions on board, Jimmie made a rough landing on the mountaintop. His plane was damaged and stuck in the mud, so they could not fly back to civilization. After 11 days, the group managed to hike out of the Gran Sabana alive. Today, Jimmie Angel's plane stands in front of the airport in Ciudad Bolivar, Venezuela, as a monument to Jimmie and his discovery.

Facts of Life

Born: August 1, 1899

Hometown: Cedar Valley, Missouri

Occupation: Bush pilot

Died: December 8, 1956

The Big Picture

Great waterfalls occur all over the world in many different climates. This map shows the locations of some of the world's highest, largest, and most beautiful falls.

ATLANTIC OCEAN

PACIFIC OCEAN

Equato

ATLAN OCEA

N
W ← → E
S

0   500   1000 1500 2000 Miles
0   500   1000 1500 2000 Kilometers

 Waterfalls

1. Angel Falls, Venezuela
At 3,212 feet (979 m), it is the highest waterfall in the world.

3. Niagara Falls, Canada/United States
More water pours over the amazing Niagara Falls than any other waterfall in North America.

2. Upper and Lower Yosemite Falls, United States
These twin falls in California's Yosemite National Park are 2,425 feet (739 m) high—the highest in North America.

4. Churchill Falls, Canada
This 245-foot (75-m) waterfall in Newfoundland, Canada, creates the energy that runs one of the largest power plants in the world.

5. Utigord Falls, Norway
Norway boasts five of the ten highest waterfalls in the world. Utigord (2,624 feet; 800 m) is Norway's highest falls and is third-highest in the world.

7. Victoria Falls, Zambia
The Zambezi River empties at this massive waterfall, which is more than 5,500 feet (1,676 m) wide.

6. Tugela Falls, South Africa
Africa's Tugela River feeds into a set of five spectacular waterfalls. Tugela (2,800 feet; 853 m) is the second-highest falls in the world.

8. Pieman Waterfall, Australia
Rising 2,346 feet (715 m) high, this waterfall is higher than any other in Australia or Asia.

People of the Tepuys

Venezuela is home to more than 300,000 indigenous peoples. In the Gran Sabana, the largest native group is the Pemón people. They came to the Gran Sabana about 200 years ago. In recent years, their population has increased as their communities have taken root in the Gran Sabana. In 1970, only about 4,000 Pemón lived there. Today, it is estimated there are as many as 20,000 Pemón in the region.

The Pemón traditionally hunt, fish, and farm. Some also have jobs as tour guides for visitors to Angel Falls.

This Pemón man knows the region well. He lives in the jungle at the base of Angel Falls.

People and the Land

Generations of Pemón people have learned much about the land near Angel Falls. They fight to **preserve** the land, too. In recent years, they showed their will by protesting against construction they believed would intrude on nature. Several times, the Pemón have knocked over new electrical lines that were built across Canaima National Park.

For many years, the Pemón have burned off plants to clear land for farms and new paths, or to rid areas of dangerous snakes. Sometimes these fires destroy sections of tropical forests. After forests are burned, savannah grasses grow back in these areas. In recent years, **environmental** scientists have worked with the Pemón to change their practice of burning land and protect the precious forests.

Most Pemón live in small villages. There are no big cities near the Gran Sabana.

Tepuy Mythology

T he Pemón people have always considered the tepuys to be **sacred** mountains. The Pemón traditionally avoided the tepuys. They believed evil spirits lived on the tepuys, and these spirits would steal human souls. Today, however, these beliefs are changing. In recent years, more Pemón live near the mountains. Frequently, they are hired by tourists to guide them through the Angel Falls area.

■ **Pemón names for tepuys reflect their traditional fear of the mountains. Auyán Tepuy means "Devil Mountain."**

Sarisarinama

Atop one of the most remote tepuys in the Gran Sabana, the Sarisarinama **sinkholes** are an awesome sight. Some of the holes appear to be perfectly circular—almost as if someone dug them out with a huge ice-cream scoop.

The indigenous peoples in this area named the tepuy "Sarisarinama," after the noise made by the evil spirit they believed lived in the mountain. That spirit says: "Sari . . . sari . . . sari. . . ."

Some of the Sarisarinama sinkholes are about 1,000 feet (305 m) deep.

Natural Attractions

Visiting Angel Falls is an unforgettable experience. The water's roar is overwhelming. Beautiful clouds of mist embrace the tepuy. Sunlight catches the mist to paint wonderful rainbows.

Traveling to Angel Falls, however, is not a simple task. Roads have not been built to allow anyone to drive from any city or town to the falls. The nearest village, Canaima, is about 30 miles (48 km) away. The rough landscape makes it too difficult for most tourists to walk to the falls. Almost all visitors arrive as part of tour groups, either by plane or by boat.

▬ **Some brave people believe the best way to experience Angel Falls is to jump off Auyán Tepuy. Parachutes are required for this extreme sport.**

Be Prepared

The Gran Sabana's **ecosystem** is fragile. When hiking in the region, visitors are instructed to stay on trails and avoid trampling plants. Visitors should never litter. No one should consider bringing home any natural wonders, such as flowers, rocks, or insects. Here are some tips for how to prepare for a trip to the region.

Always visit Auyán Tepuy with a local guide who knows the area well.

Pack everything in waterproof bags if approaching by boat.

Bring water bottles, and drink water frequently.

Rub garlic on your legs to ward off snakes, or wear shin-high boots.

Wear sunscreen and insect repellent.

Bring a compass and a flashlight.

Of course, bring a camera.

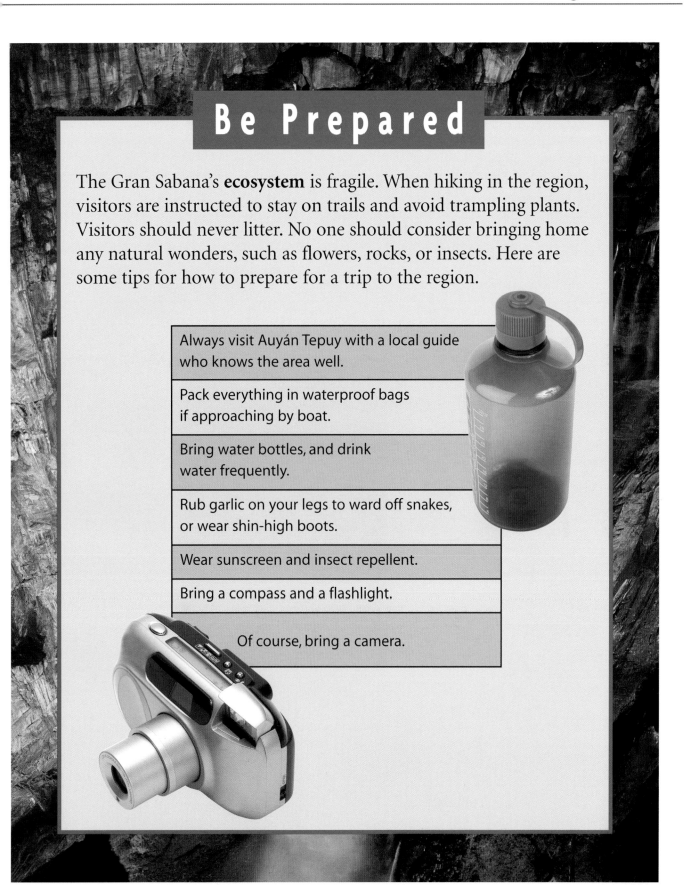

Too Many Visitors

Canaima National Park faces many environmental threats. Perhaps the largest threat is its visitors. The number of tourists in Canaima is on the rise. Officials estimate that more than 100,000 people visit every year. Although most park visitors try to be responsible guests, they can damage the environment unintentionally.

People who walk off trails can trample plants that are important to ecosystems. Rock climbers chip away at rock formations that are both beautiful and important to the landscape. Planes and boats that bring people to Angel Falls create both air and water pollution.

Visitors have been coming to the Gran Sabana for less than a century. However, they have already caused serious environmental damage.

Perhaps the greatest problem created by visitors is the garbage they leave behind. Think about the kinds of trash that tourists and campers could leave behind, such as paper, plastic bottles, metal objects that rust, and batteries that leak chemicals. During a 1999 cleanup of Roraima Tepuy, about 800 pounds (363 kilograms) of trash were collected. That is an astonishing amount of garbage, considering that the mountain is so far away from civilization.

Should the government limit the number of tourists in Canaima National Park?

YES	NO
The park is huge and employs only about a dozen park wardens. That is certainly not enough to police all the visitors.	The area is one of the world's great wonders. Everyone should be allowed to enjoy it. 
The Pemón are not accustomed to dealing with outside visitors. 	Tourists bring money to the local people in a place where there are few other economic opportunities.
Tourists leave litter, make too much noise, trample plants, and hurt precious topsoil.	Some visitors are respectful of nature. Visiting the area may increase their desire to protect the environment.

Time Line

180 million years ago
The South America continent separates from Gondwana.

3–4 million years ago
Tepuys take shape in the Gran Sabana region.

9,000 years ago
The first humans begin living in the Gran Sabana region.

1700s
The Pemón people first arrive in the Gran Sabana.

1780s
A **missionary** traveling in the region is the first visitor to report the existence of tepuys.

1884
British explorers become the first people to climb the Roraima Tepuy, the area's highest mountain.

1912
Sir Arthur Conan Doyle is inspired by stories of the tepuys and writes his bestseller *The Lost World*.

Animals in the Angel Falls region should be on the lookout for the anaconda. This snake is so strong that it crushes its prey to death.

Jimmie Angel's plane was stuck in the mud atop Auyán Tepuy for 33 years. In 1970, it was moved to Ciudad Bolivar.

1929
Explorers from Europe first use the name "Gran Sabana" to describe the region.

1933
Airplane pilot Jimmie Angel sees Angel Falls for the first time from the air.

1937
Angel Falls is named after Jimmie Angel.

1937
Jimmie Angel and several companions land their plane on Auyán Tepuy, then have to hike back to civilization.

The Canaima National Park features many beautiful waterfalls in addition to Angel Falls.

iant anteater is an inhabitant of the Gran Sabana region.

1956
Jimmie Angel dies. His ashes are scattered over the falls.

1962
Canaima National Park is established.

1970
The Venezuelan Air Force rescues Jimmie Angel's airplane from the top of Auyán Tepuy.

1994
Canaima National Park is named a World Heritage site by the United Nations Educational, Scientific, and Cultural Organization (UNESCO).

1998 and 1990
The Pemón people make worldwide headlines by attempting to block the installation of power lines intended to cross the Canaima National Park.

1999
During a cleanup on Roraima Tepuy, participants find about 800 pounds (363 kg) of garbage.

1939
The Venezuelan Ministry of Development funds the first major exploration of the Gran Sabana.

1949
Ruth Robertson leads an expedition that reaches Angel Falls. She becomes the first person to accurately measure the falls.

What Have You Learned?

True or False?

Decide whether the following statements are true or false. If the statement is false, make it true.

1. The name Angel Falls came about because the waterfall reminds people of heaven.

2. It rarely ever rains in the Gran Sabana.

3. Hundreds of species of orchids grow in the Gran Sabana.

4. Capybaras are the world's largest rodent.

5. Visitors can drive to see the falls.

ANSWERS

1. False. The waterfall is named for Jimmie Angel.
2. False. It rains a great deal during the rainy season.
3. True.
4. True.
5. False. There are no roads leading to the falls.

Short Answer

Answer the following questions using information from the book.

1. What was Jimmie Angel looking for when he found Angel Falls?

2. What is the name of the national park where Angel Falls sits?

3. In what year were the falls first measured?

4. Who was the first person to measure Angel Falls?

5. What famous adventure novel is set in the tepuys of the Gran Sabana?

ANSWERS
1. Gold
2. Canaima National Park
3. 1949
4. Ruth Robertson
5. *The Lost World* by Sir Arthur Conan Doyle

Multiple Choice

Choose the best answer for the following questions.

1. Where is Angel Falls located?
   a) Brazil
   b) Guyana
   c) Mexico
   d) Venezuela

2. What is the shape of the top of a tepuy?
   a) flat
   b) round
   c) pointed
   d) zig-zagged

3. In what region does Angel Falls lie?
   a) the Maracaibo Lowlands
   b) the Northern Mountains
   c) the Rocky Mountains
   d) the Guayana Highlands

4. Which waterfall is the second-highest in the world?
   a) Niagara Falls in North America
   b) Tugela Falls in South Africa
   c) Victoria Falls in Zambia
   d) Yosemite Falls in the United States

ANSWERS
1. d, 2. a, 3. d, 4. b

Find Out for Yourself

Books

Donnelly, Andrew. *Waterfalls.* Chanhassen, MN: The Child's World, 1999.

Shields, Charles J. *Venezuela.* Philadelphia: Mason Crest Publishers, 2004.

Wardrope, William. *Venezuela.* Milwaukee: Gareth Stevens Publishers, 2003.

Web Sites

Use the Internet to find out more about the people, plants, animals, and geology of Angel Falls and the Gran Sabana.

The Latin American Aviation Historical Society
www.laahs.com/art41.htm
Find out all about Jimmie Angel and his discovery of Angel Falls.

The Living Edens: The Lost World
www.pbs.org/wnet/nature/lostworld
Find a great deal of information on Angel Falls and the area, plus take the Eco Explorer Challenge.

The Lost World
www.thelostworld.org
This site explores the people, geography, and environment of Gran Sabana with wonderful photographs and interesting text.

Skill Matching Page

What did you learn? Look at the questions in the "Skills" column. Compare them to the page number of the answers in the "Page" column. Refresh your memory by reading the "Answer" column below.

SKILLS	ANSWER	PAGE
What facts did I learn from this book?	I learned that Angel Falls is the highest waterfall in the world.	4
What skills did I learn?	I learned how to read maps.	5, 9, 16–17
What activities did I do?	I answered the questions in the quiz.	28–29
How can I find out more?	I can read the books and visit the web sites from the Find Out for Yourself page.	30
How can I get involved?	I know that littering can damage delicate environments such as the Gran Sabana.	24–25

Glossary

carnivorous: animals or plants that feed on animals

ecosystem: a group of living plants, animals, and their environment, all of which act as a community

environmental: having to do with natural surroundings, such as climate, land, and water

eroded: worn away, slowly reduced in size

expeditions: journeys or trips made for a purpose, such as to explore a new area

geologists: scientists who study rocks, soils, and minerals

indigenous: native to a certain place; having been born in a place

minerals: substances that are neither animal nor vegetable, usually found in the ground

missionary: a person who travels to a place in order to convince the local inhabitants to join a religion

preserve: to save for the future, to shield from destruction

sacred: spiritual, religious, and holy

savannah: a grassland that is mostly treeless

sinkholes: hollow places that appear in a solid area of soil or rock

species: a specific group of plant or animal that shares characteristics

tectonic plates: large pieces of Earth's crust

Index